CIVIL WAR BATTLEFIELDS

A Photographic Journey

TEXT AND CAPTIONS: **Bill Harris**

PHOTOGRAPHY: **CLB Publishing, Godalming**

DESIGN: **Teddy Hartshorn**

DIRECTOR OF PRODUCTION: **Gerald Hughes**

CLB 3242
© 1994 CLB Publishing, Godalming, Surrey, England
All rights reserved
This 1994 edition is published by Crescent Books,
distributed by Random House Value Publishing, Inc.,
40 Engelhard Avenue, New Jersey 07001.
Random House
New York • Toronto • London • Sydney • Auckland
Printed and bound in Malaysia
ISBN 0 517 10054 1
11 10 9 8 7 6 5 4 3 2

CIVIL WAR BATTLEFIELDS

A Photographic Journey

Text by
BILL HARRIS

CRESCENT BOOKS
NEW YORK • AVENEL, NEW JERSEY

Civil War battles can confuse even the most conscientious history students. Just when they grasp that the Union army won a close victory at Murfreesboro, Tennessee, on the last day of 1862, they read that Yankee artillery turned the tide of a battle called Stones River, also in Tennessee, on the same day. It was the same battle. In the South, it was customary to name battlefields for the nearest town, but the Union army preferred the name of the closest landmark, usually a river or a creek. The bloodiest single day of the war was in a battle known as Antietam to General George McClellan's troops, but the men who followed Robert E. Lee into Maryland called it Sharpsburg. And the first important battle in the West was remembered as Shiloh by the Confederate veterans, but to General Ulysses S. Grant's Army of the Tennessee, it was called Pittsburg Landing.

The difference of opinion about what to name the battlefields might have had its origins in the Confederate capital at Richmond. It had become apparent that the Union army's primary objective was to put the city under siege, and that the first blow would probably be struck along the banks of the Bull Run, a small tributary of the Potomac River. Worried that such a name would seem unrefined, a decision was reached among the Southern leaders to refer to the battle site as Manassas for the important road and railway junction that the fighting was all about. But if there was a difference of opinion about the name, both sides agreed that it would be the site of the Civil War's first major confrontation.

The Confederate general P.G.T. Beauregard, given the job of defending the junction, wrote, "If I could only get the enemy to attack me ... I would stake my reputation on the handsomest victory that could be hoped for." As the commander of the Confederate forces that took Fort Sumter and a hero of the Mexican War, Beauregard's credentials were impeccable. His commander-in-chief, President Jefferson Davis, a West Point graduate and former secretary of war whose own military instincts were highly regarded, backed his field-commander's assessment to the hilt. Confederate strategists were all in agreement that the anticipated, decisive, early victory in what they regarded as a war for independence would encourage England and France to come to their aid and tip the balance in their favor. On the other side of the Potomac, public opinion concentrated on the importance of taking Richmond quickly, demoralizing the South and settling their differences in a single bold stroke. There was no doubt on either side that victory was in the air, but the outcome of the battle proved all of them wrong and changed the three-month-long, quiet little rebellion into a bloody war that no one, even in their most terrifying nightmares, had been able to foresee.

The thirty-five thousand Federal troops who marched out of Washington in the direction of Manassas Junction were nearly all inexperienced men, many of whom were nearing the end of their ninety-day enlistments. Their general, Irvin McDowell, a graduate of West Point who had taught tactics at the Military Academy, knew very well what a handicap he had been handed. However, when he protested to President Lincoln that he needed time to turn his men into a fighting machine, the president reminded him that Beauregard's army was also untrained. "You are all green alike," he pointed out. But McDowell's men were at a disadvantage as they had to march nearly twenty-five miles in the July heat before engaging the enemy.

They stepped off smartly enough to the sounds of military bands and the adoration of the women they were leaving behind them, but not far down the road their columns began to unravel. In spite of the sergeants' yelling, swearing, and threatening, the orders to close ranks fell on deaf ears and the gaps between units became dangerously wide. Then, in order to close up, the men were forced to march double time, and when they did get back into formation, they had to stop for long periods to wait for the dust to settle. While they were running, many of the soldiers tossed their equipment aside to lighten their load, and when they halted they munched on the rations that were intended to last them through the upcoming battle. General McDowell was appalled. "They stopped every moment to pick blackberries or get water," he wrote, "they would not keep in the ranks, order as much as you pleased. When they came where water was fresh, they would pour the old water out of their canteens and fill them with fresh water. They were not used to denying themselves much." Discipline was made even harder by the fact that the column was followed by a long line of carriages carrying Congressmen and their wives and daughters, as well as other members of the Washington gentry and a gaggle of correspondents from dozens of newspapers. The civilians gave the affair the air of a country picnic rather than a march into battle and many of them were carrying tickets for a grand victory ball at Richmond. They didn't doubt for a minute that the event was only a few days away.

McDowell's men reached Centerville, their planned destination, a day late, and when it was discovered that none of them had any rations left, another day was lost while they were resupplied, delays that gave Beauregard an extra two days to prepare for the battle. Thanks to an unexpectedly efficient spy system Beauregard knew exactly what he was facing and took advantage of the extra time to beef up the strength of his army with reinforcements, making the numbers on both sides about equal. By the time the shooting began in earnest on Sunday morning, July 21, 1861, a Union division had already engaged the enemy, with heavy losses, and some disillusioned soldiers, taking advantage of the technicality that their three-month enlistments had expired, were counter-marching in a northerly direction.

It was a great morale booster for the Confederate defenders but, as Lincoln had pointed out, they were all green troops and although both McDowell and Beauregard had devised plans patterned on Napoleon's successes, neither leader had the experienced officers or men to pull them off. The Union troops managed to cross Bull Run and drive the defenders back. However, the Confederate Brigadier General Thomas Jackson who, it was said, stood "like a stone wall," rallied the men behind his Virginians, and with fresh troops who had just arrived by train counterattacked, silencing two Union batteries in the process. Seeing that his attack was failing, McDowell sounded the call for retreat. It was orderly enough at first, but as the soldiers reached the main road, many already in a state of panic, they found the way blocked by the carriages that had followed them down from Washington and the civilians who had seen their battlefield picnics interrupted by a battle that wasn't quite going according to plan, and wanted nothing more than to get out of there themselves. It was one of the worst traffic jams in history, and certainly the most terrifying. One of the reporters who was part of it told his readers that, "For three miles, hosts of Federal troops were fleeing along the road, but mostly through the lots on either side. Army wagons ... and private carriages choked the passage, tumbling against each other amid clouds of dust and sickening sights and sounds. Hacks containing unlucky spectators of the late affray were smashed like glass and the occupants were lost sight of in the debris ... Who ever saw such a flight?"

In the meantime, early reports to Washington from the battlefield had been upbeat, and the whole city was celebrating what appeared to be certain victory when a late afternoon telegram informed officials of the retreat with the words, "the day is lost." The war itself, in fact, might have been lost that day, too, but the Confederates didn't pursue the retreating enemy. Stonewall Jackson told his superiors that with five thousand men he could easily destroy all that was left of the Union army, and he may have been right. But the men who could have followed him were exhausted and disorganized and their victory seemed quite enough for one day.

As far as the people of the South were concerned, ultimate victory was assured anyway. Everyone concurred when their newspapers told them that "one Southerner is equal to five Yankees." What they didn't realize was that Yankees by the thousands were having a change of heart over what this war meant to them. Before the shocking debacle in Virginia, the common perception had been that it was an irritating little rebellion that would be over in a matter of weeks. As weary soldiers trudged back into Washington it became obvious that this was a real war after all. And, like the attack on Pearl Harbor eighty years later, the defeat created a surge of patriotism and public support. Even as the retreat was still in progress, Congress unanimously passed a resolution that made it all quite clear: "Resolved, that the maintenance of the Constitution, the preservation of the Union, and the enforcement of the laws, are sacred trusts which must be executed; that no disaster shall discourage us from the most ample performance of this high duty; and that we pledge to the country and the world the employment of every resource, national and individual, for the suppression, overthrow and punishment of rebels in arms."

President Lincoln's first move was to demote Irvin McDowell to division commander and to replace him as head of the Federal Division of the Potomac with General George B. McClellan. McClellan had recently defeated the Confederates at Rich Mountain in Virginia, securing the territory that would eventually become the state of West Virginia. He was a popular choice, regarded as a brilliant commander by just about everyone, not least himself. When he went into battle he took a printing press along to make sure that the folks back home appreciated his accomplishments. In addition to replacing the commander, Lincoln also sent the ninety-day soldiers home and issued a call to the states to provide him with men willing to serve for at least three years. The response was overwhelming, and when the new recruits began reporting for duty, President Lincoln had a real army to help turn things around. The first and most obvious advantage was that they would all wear the same uniform. At Bull Run, the men represented state militia units and few units were dressed alike, making it difficult to tell friend from foe and resulting in many victims of what modern military people call friendly fire. But the change was more than just cosmetic. McClellan saw the need for military discipline, and for months his men drilled and marched and, although they had yet to see a battle, they slowly developed into what appeared to be crack fighting units. To the general's credit, his men seemed to love every minute of it. As one of them wrote to his family, "I never done anything yet that I like as I do soldiering." But soldiering and fighting aren't quite the same thing, and while McClellan's men were drilling on the parade ground, the Union armies in the West were engaged in battle. The problem was that hardly anyone noticed. Following a defeat at Wilson's Creek in Missouri a few weeks after the retreat from Bull Run, they were driven back a hundred miles in the direction of St. Louis. The Union's losses, about a quarter of the combatants, compared to ten percent at Bull Run, were of little interest to the folks back home, and it wasn't until nearly six months later, in February 1862, that anyone seemed to realize that this war was being fought anywhere but in Virginia.

The events that made them sit up and take notice were a quick naval victory at Fort Henry on the Tennessee River, followed immediately by the three-day siege at Fort Donelson on the Cumberland River at Dover, Tennessee. When the Confederates finally announced their intention to surrender Donelson, they invited the commander of the Union force to send a party to negotiate terms, but instead they were sent a terse message: "No terms except an unconditional and immediate surrender can be accepted." After retorting that the demand was "unchivalrous and ungenerous," they surrendered anyway and gave up fifteen thousand prisoners as well as forty-eight pieces of artillery and other weapons they could ill-afford to lose. The victory also gave the Federals a foot-hold in Kentucky and much of Tennessee, including Nashville, not to mention a bona fide hero in the person of the brigadier general who had called for unconditional surrender, a short, rumpled man named Ulysses S. Grant.

Meanwhile, McClellan's men were still marching and counter-marching in Washington. No one seemed able to make this leader move against the enemy, not even President Lincoln himself. When the president appeared at McClellan's headquarters, he was left cooling his heels for half an hour while the general attended to more important things, only to be sent back to the White House by an aide who informed him that McClellan had gone to bed. The next morning, Lincoln began studying the arts of war himself and took on the job of commander-in-chief in fact as well as in name. McClellan saw the writing on the wall and finally agreed to march on Richmond. But, rather than choosing the obvious overland route, he decided to load his men on ships, sail them down the Potomac to Chesapeake Bay, and land them on the Virginia Peninsula between the York and James rivers. From there he planned to make a short overland march and take Richmond from the east. The fact that such a move would leave Washington unprotected either from Richmond itself or from the Shenandoah

Valley didn't seem to faze the man known as the Young Napoleon. But as he assembled his armada in the river, a great many Washingtonians, including Mr. Lincoln, were scratching their heads in disbelief.

McClellan's troops had no sooner begun their march up the peninsula when they came upon a small Confederate defensive position. There weren't many defenders there, but by marching his men in a loop that made it appear to anyone outside that there were hundreds, the general in charge managed to fool the Young Napoleon, who halted his men and ordered them to begin building fortifications. Once again, the Union troops were bogged down far short of their objective, and up in Richmond, Robert E. Lee, Confederate President Davis' military advisor, was taking advantage of the extra time to shore up his defenses and redeploy his army. McClellan, meanwhile, sent a message to his commander-in-chief asking for reinforcements. He claimed that he was facing an army of "probably not less than 100,000 men and probably more." His message also said that his own force numbered only eighty-five thousand, to which Lincoln responded that McClellan had sailed down the river with fifteen thousand more than that and, even so, the enemy "will gain faster by fortifications and reinforcements than you will by reinforcements alone." The president concluded his message to the commander with the words, "you must act." And act he did; McClellan spent the next month preparing for a siege at Yorktown, still sixty miles from his goal. But on the day the bombardment was ready to begin, the Confederates evacuated, leaving him empty-handed. And in the time it took to build the fortifications in front of the town, the Confederates were building a series of roadblocks behind it, delaying McClellan's advance even more.

Even if this plan seemed flawed, there was a bright side. The Union's capture of Yorktown and Williamsburg forced the Confederates to abandon Norfolk, the home base of their ironclad vessel, *Merrimac*, which had fought the Union Navy's *Monitor* to a standoff at Hampton Roads on March 9, a week before McClellan's armada began sailing past. With the loss of their deepwater base, her crew ran the ironclad aground and set fire to it, giving the ground troops the advantage of Union naval access to the James River. But if the Union controlled the peninsula, Richmond was still in Confederate hands two months after the march toward it began.

In the meantime, Stonewall Jackson was keeping Union armies on edge in the Shenandoah Valley and prevented reinforcements from reaching McClellan, who was dug in near enough to Richmond that "his men could set their watches by the chiming clocks" there. Jackson's army of thirty-five thousand eventually reached the Confederate capital, and a day later, on June 26, 1862, Robert E. Lee, who had just become Commander of the Army of Northern Virginia, decided the time was right to attack the attackers. His main thrust was at McClellan's right wing, leaving only two divisions between the Union's main force and the city itself, but the Young Napoleon once again miscalculated the enemy's strength and, convinced he was outnumbered two to one, he called for a retreat back down toward the peninsula. By the time the fierce fighting slowed two days later, McClellan had wired his superiors in Washington begging for fresh troops. "I have lost the battle because my force was too small ... I am not responsible for this," he complained. But the battle wasn't over yet. When Lee realized that his enemy was retreating, he took it as an opportunity to destroy the fleeing army and, he hoped, end the war. The carnage that followed, remembered as the Seven Days' Battle, beginning at Mechanicsville and ending at Malvern Hill, cost Lee twenty thousand casualties and McClellan sixteen thousand. But, numbers notwithstanding, the Young Napoleon retreated to Harrison's Landing, about fifteen miles away. Before much longer he was back in Washington, and soon after was relieved of his post as general-in-chief, to be replaced by Henry Halleck, who had been in command of the armies in the West.

Halleck himself was replaced in the Mississippi region by U.S. Grant, the hero of Fort Donelson. But the man whose nickname had become "Unconditional Surrender" was by then being portrayed in the press and among ordinary citizens as a lazy drunk, unworthy of commanding even a battalion. Even the governor of his home state of Ohio had disowned him, suggesting that Grant really came from Illinois. Only President Lincoln seemed to have any confidence in him. When pressure was put on Lincoln to cashier the general rather than promote him, the president said, "I can't spare this man, he fights." The downward turn in Grant's popularity came during the battle of Shiloh, ironically a pivotal engagement won by his Union forces.

Grant's army was camped near the Shiloh Methodist Church, on the west bank of the Tennessee River, waiting for the Army of the Ohio to join them for an attack on the railway junction at Corinth, Mississippi. On the morning of April 6, 1862, Confederates, commanded by General Albert Sidney Johnston, mounted a surprise attack. Grant was, indeed, caught napping, and although his men didn't panic, the attackers managed to rout them in a series of savage attacks. The Union forces were overwhelmed, but Grant was able to establish a defensive line around Pittsburg Landing, where the fresh troops were arriving. Still, by nightfall the attackers had driven the Union army back three miles, destroyed a whole division, and severely mauled the other four in Grant's command, and had taken all five camps with their valuable ammunition and supplies. The Union troops, augmented by reinforcements, managed to turn the tide and drive the Confederates back the following day, and late in the afternoon General Beauregard, who had taken command after Johnston was killed, ordered a retreat. More than 100,000 men were engaged in the battle, and when it was over nearly 3,500 of them were dead. Union losses – killed, wounded, or missing – amounted to 13,047, and Confederate losses totaled 10,694. Although Grant took a beating in public opinion for his lack of preparedness, Shiloh was a major victory. It ended the enemy's chances of regaining western Tennessee and before long they would lose the entire Mississippi Valley.

But at the time there was no cheering in Washington or anywhere else in the North. There had been victories to celebrate, but Grant himself summed up the national mood when he said, "Up to the battle of Shiloh I, as well as thousands of other citizens, believed the rebellion against the Government would collapse suddenly and soon if decisive victory could be gained over any of its armies. Donelson and Henry were such victories ... But when Confederate armies were collected which not only attempted to hold the line further south ... but assumed the offensive and made such a gallant effort to regain what had been lost, then, indeed, I gave up all idea of saving the Union except by complete conquest." The question was how, and in the opinion of most armchair observers, the answer was where it had been all along, on the road to Richmond.

The people of Richmond saw things differently. Most Southerners also believed that complete conquest was going to end the war, and there was a strong conviction that the North had lost its will to fight, which made the conquest not only possible, but imminent. The man who would do the job, they believed, was Robert E. Lee, who had proved his mettle by driving McClellan's army away from their capital. Late in the summer of 1862, that army, 120,000 strong, was on the move northward, and at the same time the newly reorganized Army of Virginia, under General John Pope, was marching south in the direction of Manassas Junction. Lee knew that if the two armies were allowed to merge he would be hopelessly outnumbered, and he sent Stonewall Jackson to engage Pope before such a thing could happen. The two armies met at Cedar Mountain, in Culpeper County. Jackson had twenty-two thousand men, compared to Pope's twelve thousand. However, both sides suffered from the intense August heat and the ultimate Confederate victory was hard-won and inconclusive. It prompted Lee himself to march north with the rest of his army to finish the job. Two weeks later, after a series of skirmishes, Jackson's men managed to cut off Pope's supply line and then moved into hiding near the site of the earlier battle at Bull Run to wait for the rest of the Confederate army as well as for the enemy.

Pope arrived first, and although Jackson was ready for him, the two armies fought to a stalemate for two hours; before darkness ended the carnage the casualty rate had risen to more than a third of the soldiers. The following day, the Union troops concentrated, to little effect, on Jackson's men, and barely noticed that Lee had finally arrived and placed Major General James Longstreet's force in position virtually to surround them. The next morning the Federals launched a massive attack, but were forced back only to face an even more massive counterattack, and by nightfall Pope's men were retreating in the direction of Washington. But Lee was determined not to let it end there. He sent Jackson in pursuit and the two armies clashed again in a pounding thunderstorm at Chantilly Junction, a battle that stopped the Confederates in their tracks, allowing the Army of Virginia to escape. The second battle of Manassas was a stunning victory for Lee, but it was a costly enterprise. The human toll was thirty-three hundred dead and fifteen thousand wounded, and the battlefield itself was a grim wasteland for decades afterward.

Second Manassas wasn't the battle to end all battles, as Lee had hoped it would be, but it gave him an opportunity to take the war to the North, and he moved immediately toward Maryland in hopes of winning the state for the Confederacy and scoring a psychological victory with Northern public opinion. In Washington, meanwhile, Lincoln was facing the same dilemma that had dogged him from the beginning: his generals all seemed to have a knack for discrediting themselves. Pope had been sent off to Minnesota to fight Indians, and the man of the hour was once again George McClellan who, in spite of his demonstrations of incompetence, still had the loyalty – even the love – of his troops, and he was given the job of reorganizing the army to meet the new threat. Although the Union effort had been hampered all along by a poor intelligence network, the spies redeemed themselves that fall by securing Lee's plan of attack, giving McClellan a huge advantage. The orders called for dividing Lee's army, with six divisions commanded by Jackson charged with taking the Federal fortress at Harpers Ferry and three, under James Longstreet, to march toward Hagerstown,

Maryland. It was a tactical error that might have allowed the Union forces to sweep down the middle and destroy their divided enemy. But McClellan wasn't a man given to quick decisions and, while he was mulling over his options, Lee, whose own spy network served him well, discovered that his plan was in enemy hands and quickly changed it with an order to Longstreet to fall back. Jackson attacked Harpers Ferry and subdued it as planned, taking more prisoners than at any other time in the war, but the battle took longer than anticipated, and by the time it was over McClellan's men were fighting their way south. The victory prompted Lee to change his plan once again. If he was to make a stand in Maryland, it would be at Sharpsburg on the banks of Antietam Creek.

The confrontation took place sooner than Lee had expected and his strength was far less than he had planned. But if he had less than forty thousand men to engage McClellan's seventy-five thousand, he had picked a good defensive position and he had complete confidence that victory would soon be his. This was not to be and as it turned out, the battle was the most important victory the Union had yet seen, but once again at great cost to both sides. On the first day, September 17, 1862, Major General Joseph Hooker's corps hit hard at the Confederate left, commanded by Stonewall Jackson. In the attacks and counterattacks that followed, both sides poured in reinforcements, but neither could claim an advantage. In less than four hours their combined casualties were more than thirteen thousand. Another Union contingent hurled itself against Lee's troops, and although the Confederates retreated, McClellan held back and the enemy was able to recover. Meanwhile, a third Union force, led by Major General Ambrose Burnside, managed to push Lee's men back toward Sharpsburg, and by mid-afternoon the Confederates seemed to be heading for certain defeat. But by the end of the day, a counter-attack by a Confederate division, led by Major General A.P. Hill, pushed Burnside's men back to Antietam Creek, and by the time the battle was halted by darkness they had lost all that they had gained. The day would be remembered as the bloodiest single day in the country's history, a record, not matched before or since, of 22,719 Americans killed, wounded, or missing. Lee stayed in position for another attack all of the following day, but the cautious McClellan, although he had fresh troops in reserve, dallied and didn't renew the battle. Under cover of darkness on the evening of the eighteenth, Lee led his men back across the Potomac into Virginia.

Although Lincoln urged McClellan to follow, the general responded with excuses. The president later wrote, "It was nineteen days before he put a man across the river. It was nine days longer before he got his army across, and then he stopped again, delaying on little pretexts of wanting this and that. I began to fear that he was playing false – that he did not want to hurt the enemy. I saw how he could intercept the enemy on the way to Richmond. I determined to make that the test. If he let them go, I would remove him. He did so, and I relieved him." McClellan reappeared in 1864 as a presidential candidate running unsuccessfully against his former commander-in-chief.

If the victory at Antietam didn't crush the rebellion, it gave President Lincoln an opportunity to broaden support for the war by issuing his Emancipation Proclamation, declaring that all slaves held in states "in rebellion" were considered free. The fact that those states were engaged in a war for their right to be free of Washington's influence made the Proclamation a moot point, but it committed the Federal effort to a bigger cause than just the preservation of the Union, and the message wasn't lost on the people of the North. It was especially well-received now that Lee's army had been driven back to Virginia.

However, with the arrival of winter in 1862 the outcome of the war was still a toss-up. As far as the Union was concerned, a new beginning was critical. In Virginia, the Army of the Potomac, now commanded by Major General Ambrose Burnside, planned to cross the Rappahannock River at Fredericksburg and engage Lee on the way to take Richmond. The Army of the Cumberland, under its new commander William Rosecrans, was slowly moving south from Nashville in the direction of a Confederate army based at Murfreesboro, near Stones River, Tennessee. And the Army of the Tennessee, under Ulysses S. Grant, based at Memphis, was planning a move down the Mississippi to take Vicksburg, then unite with Union forces that already held New Orleans to assure complete control of the river.

But, as had happened before, the best-laid plans of the Union war effort didn't work out. Burnside was thwarted when bridge-building engineers got lost on the way to Fredericksburg, and he wasted two weeks waiting for them. By the time they started bridging the Rappahannock, Lee's men were waiting for them on the other side. Burnside lost twelve thousand men on the first day and Lee, whose losses were negligible by comparison, hadn't budged. The two armies glared at each other across the river for two days before Burnside ordered his men to head for home, and the taking of Richmond was postponed once again. Burnside was fired and the army taken out of action for the rest of the winter.

In Tennessee, Rosecrans met the enemy at Murfreesboro, and when the battle was over, the Confederate General Braxton Bragg claimed victory, although his troops had retreated. Rosecrans, whose troops were too badly mauled to follow the fleeing enemy, also claimed he had won, but both generals had lost well over a quarter of their armies and neither was able to say that the contested victory advanced the cause of either side. At the same time Grant was determined to take the Confederate stronghold at Vicksburg, and although he later wrote that "there was nothing left to be done but to go forward to a decisive victory," and the Union was desperate for such a victory, there was plenty left to be done. It took him the rest of the winter to get ready for the attack.

Vicksburg was one of those objectives that give generals ulcers. The city is on a high bluff overlooking a hairpin curve of the Mississippi; the land on either side is a flood plain filled with creeks and bayous, and the only high ground was, at the time, defended by heavy artillery. Both above and below it, for more than twenty miles, Confederate guns were poised to blow any Union boats out of the water. Still Grant believed he could take Vicksburg and, after spending the winter digging canals and rearranging creeks, he decided the only way was to run the gauntlet on the river itself. After creating a diversion to the north, he marched his men down the river's west bank and waited for the Union fleet. It arrived under cover of darkness on April 16, 1873, and although two boats were destroyed, no soldiers were lost and Grant was in a position to begin his battle. He crossed the river on April 30 and was ready to march on the city from the south, but in a bold move that would allow him to capture Vicksburg's defenders as well as the city itself, he swung around to approach it from the east. The plan flew in the face of every established military rule – his men were not only outnumbered but were surrounded on three sides, completely cut off from any lines of supply – but Grant persisted, and in spite of heavy losses he was in a position to attack. His first three assaults were beaten off, but Grant knew that time was on his side and settled in for a siege. In getting this far, his armies had won impressive victories, taking not only Jackson, the capital of Mississippi, but also destroying arsenals and capturing thousands of men along with tons of armament. "They were beaten in detail by a force smaller than their own, upon their own ground," said General Grant, and suddenly newspapers in the North began noting that this man might not be an incompetent after all.

The siege lasted from May 19 until July 4, when John Pemberton, the garrison commander, surrendered his army with a pledge that none of them would fight again. With the fall of Vicksburg the Union gained control of the Mississippi, and in the process Grant had destroyed an army of forty thousand, a loss the Confederacy couldn't afford. And, ironically, on the same day the South was reeling from an even more terrible defeat a thousand miles away near a little town in Pennsylvania known as Gettysburg.

Earlier in the spring, Major General Joseph Hooker, who had assumed command of the Union Army of the Potomac, marched into Virginia to pick up where Burnside had left off in the debacle at Fredericksburg. Hooker's plan was to leave a third of his men on the Rappahannock and establish the rest in a position to attack Lee from the rear, and since he outnumbered the enemy by more than two to one, he anticipated an easy victory. After digging in at Chancellorsville, he sent cavalry to cut off the railroad to the south, but at the same time Lee ordered "Jeb" Stuart and his cavalry to cut off the roads and, in the process, lines of communication that would allow Hooker to know where the enemy was. The major general found out late in the day on May 2, when Jackson's men pounded his flank and forced his army out into the open, where they were literally ripped to pieces. Eventually Hooker, whose army had been beaten by a force half its size, followed the familiar route back toward Washington. Lee had won a brilliant victory – although he lost the valuable services of General Jackson, who was killed in the fighting – and he decided to follow this up with a counterpunch in the enemy's own territory.

While Lee was marching toward Pennsylvania, he dispatched Jeb Stuart and his cavalry to ride around Hooker's army to keep him informed of Union troop movements. But Stuart was driven far to the east and was out of touch for more than a week, during which time the Union army, now commanded by Major General George Meade, had massed near Frederick, Maryland, much too close for comfort, forcing Lee to regroup at Gettysburg, where Meade met him on July 1. Lee pounded the smaller Union force and drove them south of the town, where they dug in along a line extending from Culp's Hill, across Cemetery Ridge and Cemetery Hill, two miles south, to a pair of hills known as Round Tops. By the morning of July 2, both armies were almost at full strength and were separated by less than a mile, with Lee's forces arrayed between the town and the Union forces, along Hanover Road and Seminary Ridge. The Confederate attack came late in the afternoon with a massive assault that shattered the center of the Union line, but by nightfall Meade had managed to secure his position. On the following day, with the advantage of the late arrival of Stuart's cavalry, Lee ordered another frontal attack, but before it could begin the attackers were driven off and the Confederates began a two-hour artillery barrage on Cemetery Ridge. By mid-afternoon they were ready to try again and twelve thousand men, led by Major General George Pickett, began charging across the open fields. They were met by withering fire, and when they were forced to fall back the Battle of Gettysburg was over. The losses were tragic – Meade had lost twenty-three thousand men, and Lee twenty-eight thousand, nearly a third of his entire army – and the Confederates were forced to march in driving rain back toward the Potomac. When they reached the river it was too swollen to cross and they waited in a vulnerable position for ten days before they could cross back into Virginia. But the Union army was too decimated to take advantage of the situation, and although the Confederacy had suffered mortal blows at Vicksburg and Gettysburg, Robert E. Lee was still a long way from raising the white flag.

The North's next main objective was the railroad center at Chattanooga and the upper Tennessee River valley. After what he had characterized as a victory at Murfreesboro, William Rosecrans was still in the area, and Braxton Bragg had moved his troops into position to protect Chattanooga. While the battle was raging at Gettysburg, Rosecrans met his enemy at Elk River, and although Bragg managed to escape he was forced to retreat more than eighty miles. Neither side sustained heavy losses, and Washington was elated by a third victory in a single week. Instead of heading for his objective, however, Rosecrans followed the retreating army, and his own troops became disorganized in unfamiliar mountain passes. Bragg, meanwhile, picked up valuable reinforcements and attacked his enemy on the banks of Chickamauga Creek, near Chattanooga itself. In the two-day battle that followed, both sides lost a third of their men. In the end Rosecrans, the clear loser this time, was sent off to St. Louis and was replaced by Major General George Thomas. Thomas, whose heroism in withdrawing the survivors behind Missionary Ridge earned him the name "the Rock of Chickamauga," had saved the Army of the Cumberland from a total disaster. The army, meanwhile, retreated into Chattanooga, but they were surrounded by Bragg's troops which held the line along Missionary Ridge in the south and east and on Lookout Mountain to the west. It was like Vicksburg all over again, but with the tables turned. As far as Bragg was concerned, all he needed to do was wait until the Yankees were starved out.

But Yankee strategy had changed. After sending more troops into the area with unprecedented speed, Washington sent General Grant to take charge. In the meantime, Bragg had thinned his own force to meet a threat posed by Ambrose Burnside's occupation of Knoxville, and when Hooker's Army of the Potomac attacked at Lookout Mountain he scored an easy victory. William T. Sherman's Army of the Tennessee made its attack farther upriver with less success, prompting Grant to send George Thomas and his men of the Cumberland to dislodge the gunners at the base of Missionary Ridge. They did as they were ordered but, in what seems to have been an effort to avenge themselves for Chickamauga, they kept on going up the steep mountain and sent the Confederates running for their lives. The fight for Chattanooga had cost the Confederacy one of its major armies as well as an important communications center. It also lost them any claim to the West and, probably most damaging of all, it gave them a formidable enemy in the person of Ulysses S. Grant, who became the only obvious choice to become commander-in-chief of all the Union armies.

When Grant went to Washington to accept the position, Mrs.

Lincoln invited him to a state dinner in his honor, but he declined saying, "I've had enough of show business." Instead, he arranged a meeting with General William T. Sherman to discuss his plan for ending the war. Both men believed that capturing cities and occupying territory was little more than a series of side shows that meant nothing as long as the Confederacy had armies in the field, and that the only way to end the rebellion was to destroy those armies. Sherman later said that Grant had decided, "He was to go for Lee and I was to go for Joe Johnston," who had succeeded the discredited Bragg as commander of the Army of Tennessee. The idea was simple: while Sherman was driving Johnston back toward Atlanta, Grant would be free to hound the Army of Northern Virginia, deprived of help. In time, if the plan succeeded, one or the other of the two Confederate armies would be defeated and Grant and Sherman would then join forces against the remaining one.

The Army of the Potomac was left in the hands of George Meade, and Philip Sheridan was brought in from the West to command the cavalry, but it was Grant who was in charge, and on May 4, 1864, he set off in the direction of the Rapidan to become the seventh general to face Robert E. Lee and his seemingly invincible army. Lee's men had been through a hard winter and they were outnumbered by more than two to one, but their general had picked a battlefield that gave them a decided advantage. As the Federal troops were picking their way through the thick underbrush and forests known, appropriately, as the Wilderness, Lee attacked. In two days, during which the woods themselves burned out of control, Grant lost seventeen thousand men and didn't gain an inch. It was a familiar scene to the veterans of other battles that always ended in defeat, but rather than the expected order to retreat, Grant urged his men to move south, not north. His plan, which also surprised the enemy, was to march all night and cut off Lee on the road to Richmond, at Spotsylvania Court House. As it turned out, Lee marched his men all night, too, and the battle that followed, one of the nastiest hand-to-hand fights in the entire war, lasted for twelve days. Four days into it, a Federal assault on the Confederate line resulted in twenty-three straight hours of close fighting in a spot that became known as "Bloody Angle." In the light of dawn, the field was seen to be littered with the dead, and an oak tree, whose trunk measured twenty-three inches around, had been hacked to pieces by rifle fire. When the fighting ended, skirmishing never stopped, and after encountering the Confederates at North Anna River, where he narrowly escaped a crushing defeat, Grant moved to the crossroads at Cold Harbor, a day's march from Richmond, determined to make a stand and bring Lee to his knees once and for all. But Lee wasn't willing to cooperate, and after ten more days of hard fighting, which cut off any hope of a direct attack on Richmond, the Union troops escaped once more in the direction of Petersburg, Richmond's railroad lifeline to the rest of the South. But Lee anticipated this move, and by the time Grant arrived there was nothing he could do but settle down for a siege. It had cost him sixty thousand men to get this far, and although he had forced the enemy to fight continuously since their first encounter at the Wilderness, Grant knew that time wasn't on his side. It was then he decided to blast his way in.

A group of Pennsylvanians who were former coal miners worked for twenty-two days digging a five-hundred-foot tunnel under the Petersburg fortifications with the idea of setting off a four-ton charge of black powder to open a hole under the city itself.

In its initial stages, the plan was to use a division of black troops to rush through the tunnel, and the men were carefully trained for the job while the digging was going on. But at the last minute, Grant, worried about the public relations fallout if the plan didn't work, substituted white soldiers to make the first assault. When the huge bomb finally exploded the untrained men panicked, and by the time they recovered, the defenders were pouring fire into the crater. More than 4,400 men died in the attempt that did little more than create a huge hole in the ground. The siege went on. It lasted well over nine months in an area of some 176 square miles, with Lee's defending army spread out over a front 35 miles long. In the six major battles involved, Grant's army of 100,000 lost 42,000 and Lee's 60,000 were reduced by 28,000. It ended on April 2, 1865, when Lee moved his troops out of Petersburg and crossed the Appomattox River on their way west. The next morning, after a battlefield meeting with President Lincoln, General Grant began leading his army in pursuit.

In the meantime, General Sherman was concentrating on Johnston's army in Georgia. With Atlanta as his goal, he managed to force the Confederates into retreat in a series of skirmishes until Johnston took a stand at Kennesaw Mountain, near Marietta. Sherman took heavy losses when he attacked the enemy who were well entrenched behind earthworks, but it was only an irritating delay and it wasn't long before the Union army was on the march again. Delay was Johnston's most powerful weapon, but it was also his undoing, and as Sherman approached Atlanta, the Confederate president Jefferson Davis replaced Johnston with General John B. Hood. Hood was a fighter, which is why he was chosen, and he chose to fight hard to save Atlanta. His first attempt, at Peachtree Creek, failed, but two days later he attacked again in what became known as the Battle of Atlanta, and he nearly saved the city before he was finally driven back. His third attempt at Ezra Church also failed, but Sherman still hadn't won his objective and wouldn't until a month later, on September 1, 1864, after a fourth battle at Jonesboro. Sherman wired his superiors, "So Atlanta is ours, and fairly won ... Since May 5 we have been in one constant battle or skirmish, and need rest." The victory came less than a month after Admiral Farragut had scored a hard-won victory in the Battle of Mobile Bay, and although Grant was still bogged down at Petersburg, spirits in the North began to soar again.

At the same time, there was also good news from the Shenandoah Valley, where Major General Philip Sheridan was carrying out Grant's orders to stop the army commanded by Jubal Early that had forced its way up the valley almost to Washington itself. Sheridan had also been ordered to destroy the rich farmland in the area, or as Grant explained it, he wanted it so thoroughly wasted that "a crow flying over the Valley would have to carry its own rations." When Sheridan thought Early had been defused, he put his men to work burning fields and barns, but Early wasn't finished yet, and he surprised Sheridan with a fierce attack on the Federal camp on Cedar Creek. What seemed like a certain Confederate victory turned to a defeat when Sheridan rallied his men and counterattacked. The brutal winter did the rest and Early was finally finished off at Winchester in late February, leaving the Shenandoah Valley firmly in Union hands. It had taken almost a full year.

While the Shenandoah was burning, General Sherman made a decision to break the Confederacy's will by marching his sixty thousand men from Atlanta to the sea, living off the land as they went, depriving the defenders of Petersburg of food and supplies. As a preview to the three-hundred-mile march, which he predicted would "make Georgia howl," he set fire to Atlanta itself. The swath he cut through the country-side was sixty miles wide and each day he sent men a few miles to each side to drive off livestock and fill wagons with all they could carry to keep their own commissary supplied. What they couldn't eat themselves, they gave to former slaves who were marching behind them, and what they couldn't carry was stolen by looters, who were also following.

Just before Sherman reached Savannah, General Hood's Confederate troops, who had moved north after the fall of Atlanta in hopes that Sherman would follow, were finally defeated near Nashville and sent into retreat. This ended any Southern hope of any more gains in the West and, with Union control of Savannah, the noose was uncomfortably tight. But the South still had a lifeline in the form of Fort Fisher, on North Carolina's Cape Fear River. It offered protection to blockade-runners who were able to move under its guns to keep the Southern war effort supplied. Obviously the hole had to be plugged, and near the end of 1864 a combined naval and ground force was sent in to do the job. The Union commander, Benjamin Butler, had earned the everlasting animosity of the South with his ruthless treatment of civilians in New Orleans, and Jefferson Davis had issued an execution order against him. Rather than putting his own neck on the line, Butler decided to blow up Fort Fisher without actually attacking it. Stripping a gunboat to make it look like a blockade runner, he loaded it with gunpowder and sent it in the direction of his target. The ship blew on schedule, but short of the mark, destroying nothing but itself. The Federals followed with a massive bombardment, the heaviest of the war, but still Fort Fisher stood, and only one defender inside was killed. The following day, Christmas Day, Butler ordered his ground troops in, but they wandered into a minefield and were forced to fall back. When captured soldiers told them that a Confederate force was moving in behind them, Butler ordered his men back to the ships and sailed away. He was replaced, of course, and two weeks later a fresh attack put Fisher out of commission, finally cutting the Confederacy off from the outside world.

At about the same time, Sherman began a new march, this time northward through South Carolina, and if Georgia had suffered, it was nothing compared to the destruction he left in the state where the rebellion began. Their destructive ardor cooled when the army reached North Carolina in March and met fierce resistance from Confederate troops determined to prevent them from reaching Grant in Virginia. But as General Johnston reported to Richmond, "I can do no more than annoy him." Although they were still willing to fight, it was becoming apparent that the Confederacy's fighting days were nearly over.

But there were still glimmers of hope. When Lee finally decided to move out of Petersburg, his plan was to take his starving men down to North Carolina, where he believed they would help Johnston stop Sherman's northward march and that the combined army could then move into Virginia to take care of Grant. Grant, meanwhile, was aware of what his enemy had in mind and moved to cut off the roads and rail lines that would allow Lee to move southward. After several days of fierce fighting the Confederate defenders were defeated. The end came on April 2, when Union troops breached the line and Lee, still hoping to link up with

Johnston, ordered the thirty thousand survivors of the siege to move out. Before leaving, he sent a message to Jefferson Davis suggesting that Richmond should be evacuated, and although the president took the advice reluctantly, he left the city with a note of optimism. "We have now entered a new phase of the struggle," he said. "Relieved from the necessity of guarding particular points, our army will be free to move from point to point to strike the enemy in detail from his base. Let us but will it, and we are free."

The next morning Federal troops entered the city of Richmond, and the prize that had eluded them from the beginning was theirs. The news electrified the North and there were victory celebrations everywhere, but the war still wasn't over.

Lee's strategy was to reach the Richmond & Danville Railroad to secure transportation into North Carolina, and with a one-day head start on Grant he thought it was possible. But when he reached Amelia Courthouse on April 3, there was no food there, and he lost his advantage with the delay for foraging. By the time they were ready to continue south, still hungry, Federal troops were barring the road. The Confederates turned west at that point, in hopes of finding supplies in the Farmville area, but wherever they went, Grant's troops were hard on their heels. Lee kept going. His supply wagons, as well as many of his men, were lost in a skirmish at Sailor's Creek on April 6, but when Grant sent him an invitation to surrender, the Virginian tersely replied, "not yet." Two days later he was forced to fight another rearguard action, but Lee was convinced that if his men could hold out until they reached Appomattox, they'd find fresh supplies and they'd be safe. But when they made their way to Appomattox Courthouse, they found Sheridan's men blocking the road. The following day, April 9, 1865, Robert E. Lee put on a fresh uniform and went to McLean House to wait for the arrival of Ulysses S. Grant.

Grant's terms were simple. The surrendering army would be paroled and their arms, ammunition, and supplies were to be confiscated. Lee accepted the terms, but made a special request that his cavalrymen and artillery troops should be allowed to keep their horses. Grant's first response was that only officers should be allowed to keep their personal property, but looking into Lee's eyes, he had a change of heart. "Let all the men who claim to own a horse or mule take the animals home with them to work their little farms," he said. All that was left to do was to put the terms in writing and sign them. That done, the American Civil War was finally over. When he left McLean House, General Lee looked long in the direction of his troops, then pounded his fist into his palm and with a quaking voice called for his horse, Traveller. He mounted Traveller and trotted, quite alone, in the direction of home.

The four-year war had ended the lives of nearly 112,000 men in the Federal Army. A further 28,000 were classified as non-battle deaths and more than 277,000 were wounded. The Confederate armies counted 94,000 battle deaths along with 195,000 victims who died of disease or as prisoners of war, and 194,000 wounded. The shooting had stopped after that short ceremony at Appomattox Courthouse and there were massive celebrations on both sides of the Mason-Dixon Line now that the carnage was over. But what no one knew at the time was that there was one more bullet to be fired, and that the last battlefield of the Civil War was to be Ford's Theater on Tenth Street, in the middle of Washington, DC.

For months before the war ended, an actor named John Wilkes Booth was obsessed with the idea of removing President

Lincoln from the stage. At first his plan was to kidnap the president and take him to Richmond, to be held as a hostage for the ransom of Southern prisoners of war. After Richmond was captured, Booth's plan changed to one of murder. Assembling a group of like-minded people, he schemed with them to kill not only Lincoln, but Vice President Andrew Johnson, Secretary of State William H. Seward, and General Grant. Booth's minions failed him, although Seward was slashed with a knife, but the assignment he reserved for himself was a tragic success.

On the morning of April 14, five days after Appomattox, Booth went to Ford's Theater, where he had been told the president would be that evening, and drilled a hole in the door of the presidential box, after which he rigged the door in the corridor so that it could be barred from inside. He reappeared there shortly after ten o'clock in the evening, not long after the third act of the comedy *Our American Cousin* had begun. At a point in the familiar play when he knew there would be only one actor on stage, Booth, who had been observing the president through the hole he had made in the door, threw the door open and fired a single shot from his derringer into Lincoln's head. Then, shouting the motto of the state of Virginia, *Sic semper tyrannis* – Thus always to tyrants – he leaped from the box onto the stage, catching his spur on the presidential flag, which caused him to stumble and break his shinbone. Booth was a well-known actor and most people in the crowded theater recognized him. But it didn't matter. He hobbled off the stage, hurried out the back door and rode off into the night in the direction of Virginia, where he expected to be greeted as a hero.

The assassin's bullet shattered Lincoln's brain, and at 7:22 A.M. the following day the president was dead. Three days later, William T. Sherman was informed of the assassination as he was about to meet with General Johnston to discuss peace. He was also warned that Lincoln's death was part of a Confederate plot, and was told that "an assassin is on your track." Without the most careful diplomacy the war could have started all over again in the face of such facts. Sherman, however, proved to be as cool and generous in peace as he had been tough and heartless in war, and at the end of his negotiations, on April 17, 1865, the war came to its formal end. Nine days later, John Wilkes Booth, who had been hidden in a barn near Port Royal, Virginia, was surrounded by cavalry troops and War Department detectives. When he refused to surrender, the troops set fire to the barn and later one of them fired on the man inside. When the dying assassin was pulled from the flames, his last words reportedly were: "Tell my mother that I died for my country." This fierce claim was symbolic of a war in which so many had died for their country.

The engine house of the old US Armory at
Harpers Ferry (left and at lower left of the
Harpers Ferry view, previous page) has been
reconstructed and is now known as John
Brown's Fort. It was where John Brown made his
final stand against Federal forces led by Col.
Robert E. Lee, sent by Washington to recapture
the town after Brown seized it in October, 1859.
Brown's capture ended his plan to arm a pre-war
slave rebellion. The town of Harpers Ferry
(overleaf) was in Virginia at the time, but since
1863 the area has been part of West Virginia.

The first shot of the Civil War was fired at 4:30 on the morning of April 12, 1861, aimed at Fort Sumter (these pages) in Charleston Harbor, one of four Federal forts, including three in Florida, in Confederate territory. After its capture two days later, it stayed in Southern hands for the rest of the war.

Fort Sumter's defenses included large-caliber, rifled Parrot guns still on display there (facing page top left and bottom) along with shells that penetrated its walls (facing page top right). Its commanding position (above) at the entrance to Charleston's harbor made Sumter the scene of several unsuccessful Union attempts to retake it.

As fighting raged around her home on the Manassas battlefield, eighty-year-old Judith Henry was carried to the safety of a ravine. She begged to be able to die in her own bed and was taken back, where she got her wish when a Union shell scored a direct hit on the Henry House (left), which has now been rebuilt.

The two battles that took place at Manassas, Va., are sometimes called the Battles of Bull Run for the creek (above) that runs through the battlefield. It was on Henry Hill (facing page) that the famous Rebel Yell was first heard when Stonewall Jackson told his outnumbered troops, "When you charge, yell like Furies."

"THERE STANDS JACKSON LIKE A STONE WALL"

*More than eight thousand Americans died in the two battles at Manassas. Their memorial is a
simple stone monument (facing page). More impressive is the one (above) that honors General
Thomas J. Jackson, called "Stonewall" after General Barnard Bee said to his men: "There is
Jackson, standing like a stone wall. Let us determine to die here and we will conquer."*

HONOR THEIR VALOR, EMULATE THE
DEVOTION WITH WHICH THEY GAVE
THEMSELVES TO THE SERVICE OF
THEIR COUNTRY, LET IT NEVER BE
SAID THAT THEIR SONS IN THESE
SOUTHERN STATES HAVE FORGOTTEN
THEIR NOBLE EXAMPLE.

The monument (facing page) to Confederate dead at Fort Donelson might also honor the twelve thousand able fighting men taken prisoner, and out of the action, after Ulysses S. Grant's first victory and his demand for the "unconditional surrender" of the garrison and its cannon (top), agreed upon at the Dover Inn (above).

The battle that took place at Pittsburg Landing (right), Tenn., is often called Shiloh for the log church that served as Confederate headquarters. The name means "a place of peace," but the men who faced the massed cannon there called part of the battlefield "The Hornet's Nest."

Shiloh is peaceful today, but when war came there as spring bloomed in 1862, bullets whizzed through the trees at Water Oaks Pond (facing page top), there were gunboats on the Tennessee River (facing page bottom), and the Sunken Road (above) was a river of mud raked with cannon fire, leaving hundreds of dead piled one on top of the other.

Union cannon (above) supported repeated charges against a well-defended peach orchard at Shiloh. The trees were in full blossom and pink petals filled the air. Also among the incongruities were the bucolic George Cabin (facing page top) surrounded by cannon (facing page bottom), and the quiet body of water (overleaf) known ever since as Bloody Pond.

Shiloh's dead are honored with a host of monuments (these pages), including what is left of the tree (left) where General Albert S. Johnston was mortally wounded.

The bombardment of Fort Pulaski (these pages) on Cockspur Island at the mouth of the Savannah River lasted thirty hours before the stars and stripes were raised over it. Its heavy guns and thick brick walls had made it seem impregnable.

*Damage from the cannonade is still quite evident in Fort Pulaski's walls (facing page top).
After Union gunners crossed the moat (above) to accept surrender, Savannah was sealed off
from the sea.*

Pulaski's cannon were no match for artillery that breached the casemates (facing page top) and the terreplain (above and facing page bottom), near the powder magazine.

Stone House (these pages) on the Manassas battlefield (overleaf) was a field hospital, though obviously not big enough. In the second battle, 15,799 men were wounded.

When George McClellan's Union troops pursued Robert E. Lee's army to Sharpsburg, Md., McClellan found them waiting in these fields (right) near Antietam Creek. He lost 13,609 men. Lee lost 14,756 in what is still remembered as the bloodiest day in American history.

The Dunker Church (left), an Antietam landmark, has a plain interior and no steeple because those of the Dunker religion shun what they see as vanity. They are also opposed to war, which reached their churchyard with a vengeance that September day in 1862. None of the buildings in the area, including the Pry House (above), were left unscathed.

A sunken farm road (above and facing page top) at Sharpsburg became "Bloody Lane" when sharpshooters broke a Union advance. The Rebels also triumphed in saving an important bridge on Antietam Creek (facing page bottom).

Antietam National Battlefield (these pages) covers three thousand acres of the Maryland country-side. In addition to memorials to the regiments that fought there, key moments of the battle are recalled through informational plaques.

Antietam's National Cemetery (facing page top and above) honors thousands who came from all parts of the North and South, never to return home. The classical Maryland Memorial (facing page bottom) honors local boys and men.

The Battle of Fredericksburg is graphically recalled in paintings displayed at Fredericksburg and Spotsylvania National Military Park in Virginia (above and overleaf). The 18th-century Chatham Mansion (facing page top) still stands at the edge of the battlefield (facing page bottom).

Lee's Hill (above and right) at Fredericksburg was Robert E. Lee's forward command post, with a view of the battle in both directions as well as of the town of Fredericksburg itself. Along with other hills surrounding the battlefield, including Prospect Hill (top right), it provided ideal artillery positions.

ERECTED
BY
PENNSYLVANIA
TO
COMMEMORATE
THE CHARGE OF
GENERAL
HVMPHREYS'
DIVISION
FIFTH CORPS ON
MARYES HEIGHTS
FREDERICKSBVRG
VIRGINIA
DEC · 13 · 1862

134TH 129TH 126TH 91ST
131ST 133RD 123RD 155TH
PENNA · VOL · INFY

BRIGADIER · GENERAL
ANDREW ATKINSON HVMPHREYS
THIRD DIVISION · FIFTH ARMY CORPS

Fredericksburg changed hands seven times during the war in four major battles. Marye's Heights, the scene of two of them, is filled with memorials (these pages), from silent cannon to gravesites to elaborate bronzes.

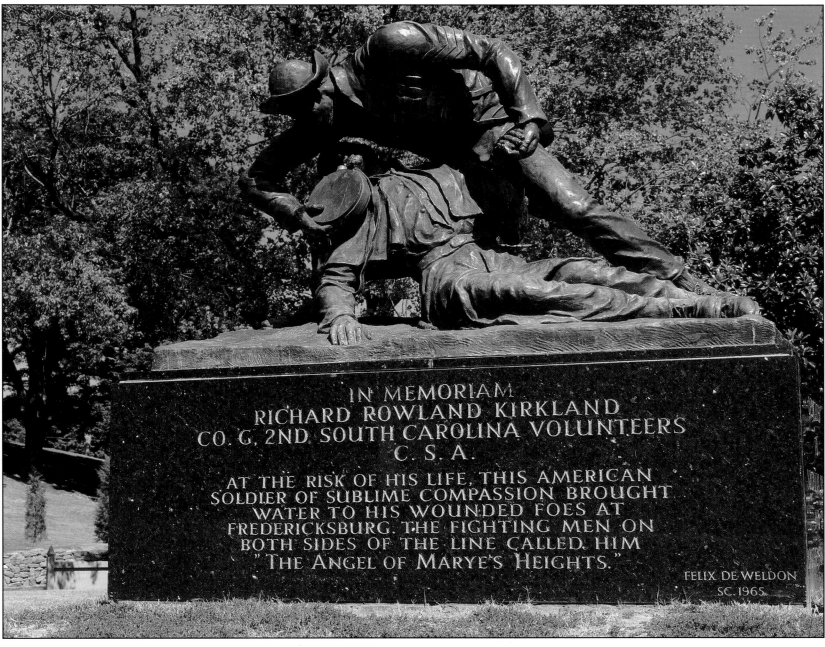

IN MEMORIAM
RICHARD ROWLAND KIRKLAND
CO. G, 2ND. SOUTH CAROLINA VOLUNTEERS
C. S. A.

AT THE RISK OF HIS LIFE, THIS AMERICAN
SOLDIER OF SUBLIME COMPASSION BROUGHT
WATER TO HIS WOUNDED FOES AT
FREDERICKSBURG. THE FIGHTING MEN ON
BOTH SIDES OF THE LINE CALLED HIM
"THE ANGEL OF MARYE'S HEIGHTS."

FELIX DE WELDON
SC. 1965

The National Cemetery at Stones River, Tenn., contains the bodies of some of the twenty-five thousand casualties suffered in two days of fighting, beginning on New Year's Eve, 1862.

When fighting began at Stones River (facing page top right), the first volley killed seventy-five horses, and Union guns were abandoned (above). After quiet had settled, neither side had won, but thirty percent of their men were left behind (overleaf). Facing page top left: the Hazen Monument at Stones River National Battlefield, and (facing page bottom) looking across Cotton Field from the edge of Cedar Thicket.

When fighting broke out at Chancellorsville, Union General Dan Sickles was at Catharine Furnace (above). The roar of cannon at Hazel Grove (facing page) prompted him to head there, and in the confusion he took losses from friendly troops.

Fighting Joe Hooker commanded the Union armies from the Chancellor House Hotel, which stood in a field now marked only by graves (above and top left). Out among his enemies was Stonewall Jackson, who was hit by friendly fire at Chancellorsville and died of his wounds. A simple monument (left) marks the spot.

Among the early assaults on Vicksburg, the USS Cairo *tried bombardment from the Mississippi, and wound up on the bottom. Her guns (left) have since been raised and are now on display where her target had been.*

Vicksburg's location above the Mississippi River (facing page bottom) saved it from naval attack. It was protected on the landward side, too (facing page top, and above). And General Grant failed time after time to win the prize.

Grant won Vicksburg's surrender after a long siege, an ordeal that is remembered by such impressive monuments as Mississippi's (above) and those of Texas (facing page top) and Illinois (facing page bottom).

Gettysburg was the Civil War's biggest battle, and Cemetery Ridge (right) its pivot point. It was here on the third day that Lt. George Pickett's men charged against the Union occupiers and were turned back, effectively ending the battle.

Among the memorials to Gettysburg's dead is the one (above) honoring Pennsylvania's regiments in the National Cemetery (right), where President Lincoln delivered his immortal Gettysburg Address in November, 1863. The tower in the background (top right) offers a view of the entire Battlefield and the town of Gettysburg (overleaf).

A tour of the Gettysburg Battlefield includes the Wheatfield (top left), where the first skirmishes took place; the Peach Orchard (left), where the overextended Yankees were routed on the second day; and the Angle (above) where Pickett's men inflicted heavy losses before being driven back from the assault on Cemetery Ridge.

The Gettysburg Battlefield is studded with memorials (facing page top, above and overleaf).
Among them is a statue of Fighting Joe Hooker (facing page bottom), replaced by George Meade at
the head of the Union Army a few days before the battle.

At one point during the Battle of Chickamauga, General William Rosecrans told his staff, "If you care to live any longer, get away from here." They did, and the Union line moved back to Brotherton House (above). Facing page top: the monument to the 15th U.S. Infantry, and (facing page bottom) the site of the Rosecrans retreat, at Chickamauga and Chattanooga National Military Park.

Among the units involved in the Battle of Chickamauga were troops from Georgia (above) and Florida (facing page). A Confederate victory, the toll was 18,450 casualties for the South and 16,170 for the North.

GARRITY'S ALABAMA BATTERY.
TWO 10 PDR. PARROTTS, TWO 12 PDR. NAPOLEONS.
MAJ. ALFRED R. COURTNEY'S ARTILLERY BATTALION.
HINDMAN'S DIVISION.
NOV. 1863.
CAPT. JAMES GARRITY, Commanding.
1st LIEUT. PHILIP BOND.
1st LIEUT. MAYWARD A. HASSELL.
2nd LIEUT. HENRY F. CARROLL.

THE SECTION OF PARROTT GUNS OCCUPIED THIS POSITION FOR NEARLY TWO MONTHS
PREVIOUS TO THE BATTLE OF THE 24TH AND WAS ENGAGED AT INTERVALS IN FIRING AT THE
ENEMY'S WAGON TRAINS IN MOCCASIN POINT BATTERIES AND LINES FACING MISSIONARY
RIDGE. ABOUT MIDNIGHT OF NOV. 23RD, AFTER THE ENEMY HAD ADVANCED AND OCCUPIED
ORCHARD KNOB THIS SECTION WAS ORDERED TO REPORT TO GENERAL ANDERSON
COMMANDING THE DIVISION WHICH THEN OCCUPIED THE LINE OF WORKS AT THE BASE OF
MISSIONARY RIDGE AND ON ITS RIGHT EAST OF ORCHARD KNOB AND NORTH OF THE
BIRDS MILL ROAD.

After the Battle of Chickamauga, General Bragg had lost the bulk of his army and all his horses. But his men had the Union forces encircled from such strategic points as Lookout Mountain (right) above Chattanooga.

In spite of his sweeping view of the river (above), Bragg missed movements at Craven House (top) nearby, and Lookout Mountain fell. Illinois units that helped take the city are memorialized there (facing page).

Generals Lee and Grant met for the first time in battle at the Wilderness (above). They met again at Spotsylvania, where the most vicious fighting of the war took place at Bloody Angle (facing page).

After driving the enemy to Kennesaw Mountain (facing page bottom and above), General Sherman's assault, recreated today (facing page top), cost him two thousand men. Confederate losses were less than five hundred men.

The siege of Petersburg, Va. left scores of craters (facing page top) and forlorn soldiers' huts (facing page bottom). It also left hundreds of ruined homes (above), and marked the beginning of the end of the Confederacy.

As the war came nearer, the Confederate capital at Richmond bristled with cannon (these pages) to protect its homes. The city surrendered before any of them were fired. Above: the Watt House at Gaines Mill.

On the morning of April 3, 1865, after President Jefferson Davis had led the evacuation of his burning capital, the cannon around it were silent, the trenches empty, the banks of creeks deserted. Then, an eyewitness said, "... a single bluejacket rose over the hill." Richmond (these pages) had fallen.

The end came in the parlor (top) of Wilbur McLean's home (above) at Appomattox Court House, Va.. Two nights later, Abraham Lincoln was assassinated in a box at Ford's Theater (facing page), in Washington. Overleaf: cannon at Petersfield.

INDEX